It's a strange state of affairs when a nine-month-old baby can't turn up in a foreign country uncontroversially, but if Prince William would be photographed cuddling a toy koala made out of kangaroo skin, raised eyebrows were inevitable. So when on Sunday 20th March 1983 he was proudly held up by his parents on arrival at Alice Springs at the begining of their month-long tour of Australia, local ears still rang with the strictures of Mrs Maryland Wilson, a member of the Victorian RSPCA, who accused those same royal parents of having "no concern for wildlife".

As if all that were not enough, Alice Springs copped a monsoonal low five days before the arrival and was at the receiving end of a record 200 mm of rainfall in three days. Three people drowned, a hundred were evacuated, trees were felled, bridges swept away

and the centre of Alice cut off for thirty hours. Worse still, the floods isolated the Casino Hotel where the Prince and Princess were to stay, and in last-minute arrangements their accommodation was transferred to the Gap Motor Hotel. After so many alarms their arrival seemed not only uncontroversial but throughly delightful. To the surprise and rapture of the crowds the Prince and Princess' formal welcoming was short on ceremony and Nanny Barbara

Barnes appeared at the top of the aircraft steps holding Prince William. She brought him down to join his parents and everyone was treated to the sight of the Princess proudly holding her baby. He squinted frantically as a bright, early-morning sun blazed down, and Prince Charles later confirmed that "his first welcomer was the ubiquitous Australian fly". With them came a party of twenty-two staff, including private secretaries, a lady-in-waiting, press and police officers, and a physician. Prince Charles brought two valets, on the grounds that "it's a twenty-four hour-a-day job" in the words of his Press Secretary, and Kevin Shanley, the Princess' celebrated hairdresser, came too. Behind them all were almost twenty four hours' flying, which left them with what Prince Charles admitted was "tertiary jet lag". Before them lay a gruelling tour of a month's duration, with only a smattering of well timed breaks. Perhaps Prince William, who was flown immediately from Alice to Woomargama, the Wales's home base for the next month, would after all come out best. No work, unsuspecting of petty controversies, and with four weeks in Australia's fair climate — this was the perfect alternative to the damp and reluctant Spring back home.

The Prince and Princess of Wales wasted no time at all in starting their busy itinerary. The very next morning, the royal couple arrived at the new St. John Ambulance Regional Centre to open the building. Despite the fact that they must still have been suffering from the inevitable jet-lag, they managed to appear bright and breezy for the occasion, the Princess wearing the lightest of bright yellow dresses. The sheer ease with which she chatted to the obligatory line of dignitaries struck everyone present. No perfunctory hand-shake and fixed smile from her. It somehow brought to mind the fact that many years ago someone had said of

the Queen Mother that she laid foundation stones as if it was the best way of spending an afternoon that she could possibly imagine.

After the opening ceremony came a tour of the building, funded by the Department of Health, and the Prince and Princess were treated to an informative inspection of an ambulance and an emergency helicopter, which had been used to rescue people stranded during the recent floods.

Later that same morning the Prince and Princess visited the Alice Springs School of the Air, which gives lessons by radio to children in remote villages. They took advantage of the system to answer children's questions.

After the broadcast the Prince and Princess met over a thousand cheering, flag-waving children outside. At one time the Princess seemed to be in danger of being swamped by the youngsters, but once again her obvious liking for young children shone through and won the day.

The Ayer's Rock area is no longer the desert it used to be. For many years it has sacrificed its former rugged glory under the name of the Red Desert to the comparative luxuriance bestowed by fifteen years of tolerably moist seasons.

Fortunately for the peace of the Prince and Princess of Wales' visit there on the 21st March, there is no dispute about its ownership — a trio of Aborigine elders, for whom it has sacred and magical connotations, have adopted its caves as places of worship and manhood initiation ceremonies.

The royal couple arrived just after 6 pm, their eight-car motorcade halting at The Climb, one of the more accessible to facilitate progress. A small cluster of memorial plaques near the bottom immortalises those who omitted to use it, and warns those who now would not.

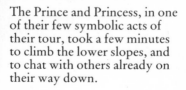

The Prince and Princess, in one of their few symbolic acts of their tour, took a few minutes to climb the lower slopes, and to chat with others already on their way down.

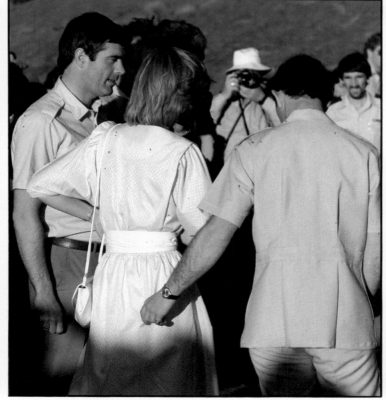

The rather tricky, steep descent from the Rock completed, the guides took the Prince and Princess to see what every tourist must —sunset on the Rock. The sunset viewing-point was well populated by the time they arrived and the Press was not long in swelling the ranks, cheering wildly as the royal couple posed for photographs against the background of the Rock. There was time for a little royal chat with the other spectators: "He wanted to know where I came from", one American woman excitedly told her friends, little suspecting the usual royal

opening conversational gambit. In those last minutes of direct sunlight the Rock changed in colour from puce to rich brown, the sun playing golden tinges and deep, black shadows among its crevices and outcrops. There was no drama, none of the oohs and aahs associated with spectacular theatrical effects. The imperceptible variations absorbed onlookers into a whispered silence until twilight came, eventually leaving the Rock —a flat, incongruous backdrop— to its natural deserted self.

to open the doors, standing bewildered in the sunshine while the Prince and Princess let themselves out. The Princess, in a fetching white and green outfit, obviously enjoyed herself during the walk up the school drive as she chatted to the children and accepted bouquets and gifts. Once in the building, the royal couple were treated to a rendering of a song entitled "But I can't spell

Early the next day the Prince and Princess flew out of Alice Springs, heading for Tennant Creek and Karguru School. When their car arrived at the school from the airport, it pulled up short, leaving the pair of boy scouts, who were meant

hippopotamus". Prince Charles hoped that, after a month's rehearsal, they could spell it now. He and the Princess then visited several of the open-plan classrooms, all sporting a colourful blend of art, local interest, history, maths and so on, and were presented with an Easter egg for Prince William. The three hundred miles from Alice Springs may have seemed a long way to come, but somehow it had not been a waste of time.

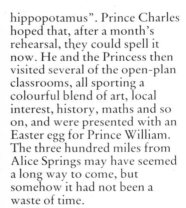

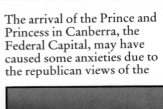

The arrival of the Prince and Princess in Canberra, the Federal Capital, may have caused some anxieties due to the republican views of the

Prime Minister Bob Hawke, but the reception from the public left nothing to be desired. Once the formalities at the airport were over, the royal couple went for a walkabout in the Civic Centre, where the cheering was loud and long. The Princess, dressed for the occasion in a high-necked and generously-skirted turquoise outfit, was clearly gratified by yet another friendly welcome.

After the tumultuous welcome at the Civic Centre Prince Charles and the Princess drove to the peaceful and elegant retreat of Australian Premiers; The Lodge. On the steps of the house, Bob Hawke welcomed his royal visitors for the second time in just three hours. After drinks had been served, the group of VIPs reappeared for a press photo-call. Prince Charles looked as confident as might be expected of one who has done this sort of thing several times before, while the Princess seemed to take her cue from him, spicing her conversation with the occasional quip which went down well even with the redoubtable Mr. Hawke. That evening the Princess of Wales wore a dazzling new evening dress, with the dropped waist she has recently favoured, to a dinner given by the Governor General. She was inevitably, but rightfully, the brightest jewel of all the forty-five guests.

Not long before the Royal Visit to Australia began, terrible bush fires swept through the area around Cockatoo near Melbourne. Thousands of acres of land had been devastated and many homes destroyed. It was this appalling toll on life, limb and property which prompted the royal visitors to cut short their trip to Canberra in order to visit the scenes of the fires. During their journey to Cockatoo the Prince and Princess drove along roads

lined with the blackened remains of forests and woods, the smoked ruins of once decent homes, and the mangled metal of burnt – out motor vehicles and tin sheds. Later, while talking to fire-fighters and victims, they heard tales of incredible heroism and of heartbreaking loss. The symbolic importance of the young tree which the Prince and Princess planted was not lost on those present, who were faced with the job of rebuilding their homes and lives.

On the 26th of March the Princess of Wales admitted that she was still suffering from the residue of jet-lag, but her problems were nothing compared to those of the 2,000 people that she and Prince Charles met at Stirling Oval in the Adelaide Hills that morning. These were some of the victims of the bushfires, and the Princess was aware of the delicacy of the situation: "I hope you don't mind the intrusion," she told one woman. While Prince Charles restricted himself to earnest conversation, the Princess was busy shaking dozens of hands and doing her best to accept the donations of gifts and flowers from small children. The royal couple then met the crews of fourteen fire-trucks, including eighteen-year-old Philip

Williams. This young volunteer fireman had become trapped by the flames and had suffered severe burns, and was now visibly and particularly impressed by the genuine concern the couple showed him. Just as the visit was ending a fireman ran up to Prince Charles and presented him with a fireman's helmet as a souvenir. In it was the inscription "From the boys of Cudlee Creek". "He seems to be one of the boys too," said the fire fighter.

On the 28th of March the Prince and Princess arrived in Sydney and were driven to the Opera House for an open air programme of music and dance put on by local schools. The Opera House forecourt was packed with ten thousand people, many of whom had bought colourful plastic flags for one dollar each. When it become known that the royal couple would be travelling in an open car all eyes were fixed in the direction of their arrival until the distant sound of cheering and the sight of waving flags proclaimed their approach. As the slow motorcade wound its way to

Two flamingoes made of lard, a koala modelled in ice and a State crest fashioned from butter were among the showpieces of an enormous table of fare, thirty metres long, laid ready for four hundred guests at Parliament House, the still uncompleted headquarters of the New South Wales legislature, where the Prince and Princess arrived amid dense lunch-hour crowds. Prince Charles invited them to "attack" the food —citing the example of Prince Alfred's banquet on the Yarra in 1867, ruined by a gang of marauding toughs. "That," he explained, "is why there are police vans outside today!"

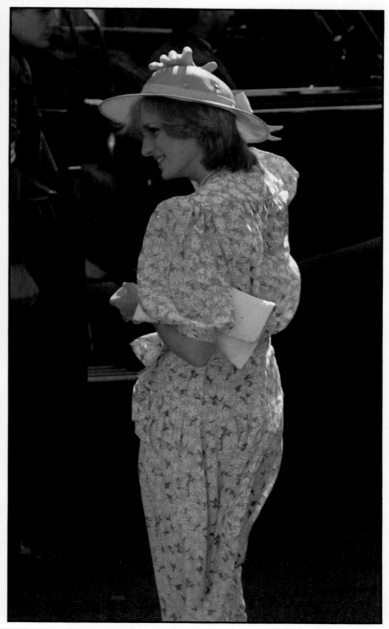

the edge of the Opera House forecourt it was pelted with flowers (one bouquet unfortunately struck the Princess in the face) and when they dismounted the supposed formal procession evaporated into yet another brief walkabout. The Princess simply cannot resist them. Before the music began Prince Charles made a speech recalling his first visit as a "hesitant Pom" seventeen years earlier, and thanked the Australians for the way his wife had been "envelopped by warmth and affection."

It seemed a little early in the year to call the ball at the Wentworth Hotel Sydney's most brilliant social event of 1983, but everyone said it was just that. A crowd gathered outside the hotel and when the Prince and Princess arrived the welcome could have been for the world's most sought after pop star, so shrill and prolonged were the cheers and so numerous the camera flashes.

The entrance of the royal couple certainly justified all the excitement before the ball. The Princess' breathtaking impact was achieved not by any grandness of manner — that is not her style — but by the sheer elegance which invariably

shines through her endearing brand of slightly embarrassed modesty. Wearing a graceful mid-blue evening dress, flounced, ruffled and with a light, generous double-skirt, she avoided the temptation of over-dressing — a gold cummerbund and a diamond necklace and earrings providing the only sparkle. Though the Prince's dancing may have been short on style the Princess seemed to enjoy it. The event proved to be the glittering success that it had promised to be, even if the royal couple did have to leave after only an hour of dancing.

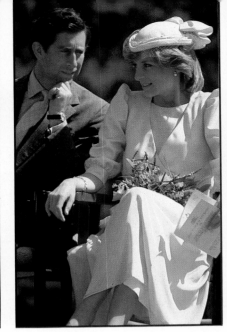

"Our ears are ringing with all the noise you made," said the Prince. The sound of 43,000 children shrieking their cheers together is an unforgettable one and the Prince and Princess of Wales' memories of their short visit to Newcastle on 29th March will be coloured by what they heard as much as by what they saw. But seeing was important too. "Don't forget to wave a the end," urged one of the rehearsal organisers patiently over the loud-speakers at the huge Oval. "We all want to see you wave to the Prince and Princess, and I'm sure the beautiful Princess Diana would like to see you wave too." And she did.

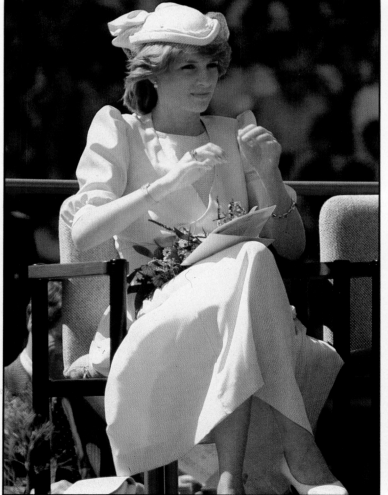

After the success of the visit to the sports ground the royal couple travelled to Maitland for another walkabout and official welcome. Unfortunately the police crowd control was not all it might have been and at one point it looked as if the vast numbers of people would get out of control. However, this did not happen and the event went ahead uninterrupted. During his speech Prince Charles expressed his wish that Prince William would visit the town some time in the future, a wish that seemed to be shared by most townsfolk.

It was perhaps unfortunate that the two-day visit to Tasmania, among the most royalist of the Australian states, should have got off to a bad start. At Hobart airport Prince Charles did not join his wife on the walkabout and many children were left without so much as a glimpse of the couple they had waited so long to see. Again at Waterman's Dock the route of the walkabout was far too short for the numbers who had arrived to cheer and some people were left feeling a little hard done by.

The controversial Franklin-below-Gordon dam issue failed to spoil the royal couple's day at Hobart on 30th March — the first of two days spent visiting Tasmania's "windy little isle" as Prince Charles called it. Its high point followed a pleasant tour of Rokeby High School, the Prince and his wife crossing the harbour from Bellrive to Waterman's Dock on the VIP launch *Egaria*. Fashion-watchers noted that the Princess' 1981 Ascot outfit lived to see another day.

The royal visit to Tasmania will, perhaps, be best remembered for an incident durign Prince Charles' speech at the official reception. Speaking of all the "Good luck" messages during his pre-wedding tour of Australia in 1981 he remarked gallantly: "I was indeed lucky enough to marry her." His wife, to whom

all eyes immediately turned, screwed her face up into a half-mocking, half-threatening glare at the Prince who spun round, too late to catch it as the assembly erupted with laughter. "It's amazing what ladies do when your back is turned," he grinned.

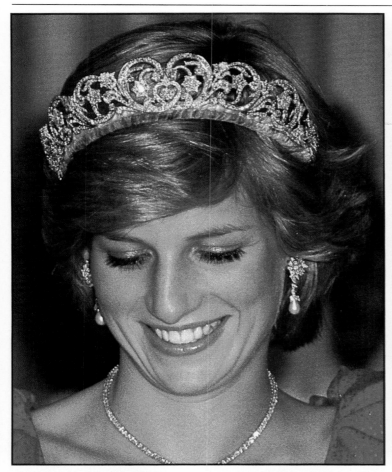

When the royal visitors left Hobart they engaged in one of the whistle-stop tours which are sometimes forced upon royalty because of the need to see so much in such a short time. They left Hobart at 9.15 am and four hours later were one hundred miles away in Launceston, having visited four towns on the way.

The first stop on the royal drive along the Midland Highway in Tasmania was the sleepy little town of Kempton. The population of this town, usually under a thousand, was swelled beyond all recognition by the large numbers of villagers from outlying districts who flocked in to see the royal couple pass. However, there was still enough room for everyone to see and with Easter just three days away gifts of Easter eggs abounded. During the brief stop in the next town, Oatlands, Prince Charles found time to congratulate Mrs. Betty

Burke, who was expecting a baby just a week before Prince William's first birthday, while the Princess was being overwhelmed by schoolchildren bearing welcome messages. Though the royal couple only stayed fifteen minutes in Ross its natural charm made a definite impression. It's beautiful", Prince Charles told a resident of Campbell Town, the next place on the programme. Another resident of the town had found out the Prince's weakness for honey and

presented him with enough to keep Winnie-the-Pooh sated for life. When the royal couple reached Launceston they visited the new A$11 million Civic Square, where they each planted a tree to commemorate their visit. The final engagement of the trip to Tasmania was a visit to the Australian Maritime College, after which the Prince and Princess returned to Woomargama for Easter.

The royal couple spent the Easter holiday at their base in Woomargama and on Easter Sunday attended the service in St. Matthews Church, Albury which, predictably, had its largest congregation for years. A capacity attendance of 350 was swelled by two hundred additional worshippers who listened to the service on an outside relay system.

Immediately after the church service Prince Charles, accompanied by his wife, travelled to Warwick Farm to play in a polo match, his first for six months. For the Princess, though, there was an ulterior motive. At the match she met Ann Bolton, her flat-mate from bachelor-girl days, who is now resident in Australia, and was able to catch

up on all the personal gossip. The Prince of Wales acquitted himself well, but his months of inactivity showed towards the end of the match. After the game the Prince was called upon by three thousand vociferous spectators to make a speech and thanked the Princess for "loyally watching her husband make a fool of himself."

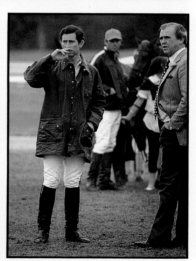

Tuesday 5th April saw the royal couple at Adelaide's Parks Community Centre, with its indoor and outdoor sporting complexes, a theatre, library and arts centre, and health, education and social welfare facilities. In a potted guided tour, they saw a display of simulated rock-climbing, table-tennis played by Vietnamese and Cambodian refugees, youngsters practising handsprings and trampolining, ladies going through their fitness-through-dance routines, and swimming tuition for the disabled.

That evening they attended a disco at Adelaide University —an event strictly for the under-forties.

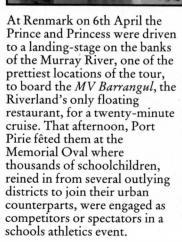

At Renmark on 6th April the Prince and Princess were driven to a landing-stage on the banks of the Murray River, one of the prettiest locations of the tour, to board the *MV Barrangul*, the Riverland's only floating restaurant, for a twenty-minute cruise. That afternoon, Port Pirie fêted them at the Memorial Oval where thousands of schoolchildren, reined in from several outlying districts to join their urban counterparts, were engaged as competitors or spectators in a schools athletics event.

Port Pirie's athletics came predictably to an abrupt halt as wild cheering greeted the royal arrival. After watching the final events, the visitors were welcomed by the Mayor in a speech which recalled that the silver used for Australia's wedding present to the Prince and Princess —twenty silver platters— had been produced in Port Pirie. They were now matched by a present of silver servers, and the Princess also accepted a small smocked suit for Prince William.
Rebecca La Forgia was one of ten pupils to receive a handsome Australia-shaped

wooden trophy from the Prince. "I hope Lady Diana doesn't mind," she asked him within the Princess' hearing, "but may I give you a kiss on the cheek?" Prince Charles looked at his wife for instructions. She hitched her shoulders in a resigned shrug of approval. Prince Charles lowered his face and the kiss was given — "more fun than receiving the trophy," said Rebecca. The Prince was obviously bucked by the compliment. His wife giggled. The crowd whooped with delight at this moment of unrehearsed good spirits at the end of a hasty visit.

Showers punctuated the
following day's proceedings,
but out came the sun as the
Princess of Wales, performing
her first solo duty of the tour,
arrived at Fremantle Hospital,
one of the few institutions in
the Commonwealth that can
boast a block named after her,
the Princess of Wales Wing.
Everyone acknowledged that
her outfit was the most elegant
and dazzling since her arrival in

Australia —a stylish, deep pink dress with white spots, and a matching pill-box hat with a huge rippling bow at the side. Many people were disappointed when her car sailed well past the original stopping-point before she alighted, but the more fortunate were thrilled to see her at her very best —much more relaxed, and giving everyone the chance ultimately to go home and truthfully say they'd seen her. She spent barely fifteen minutes in the building— enough only to tour a few wards and speak to half-a-dozen patients.

The royal couple joined forces for a trip to Perth's Commonwealth Hockey Stadium —a blaze of colour with its brilliant green artificial turf, tangerine-hued chairs and terraces crammed with children forming a herbaceous border of brightly-coloured uniforms. A wash of cheers greeted their arrival and their triumphal open-car tour of the ground, and children unable to present flowers to the Princess personally simply hurled them, with remarkably good aim, into

the car. When she actually caught one bouquet in mid-air she was cheered as if she had just scored a century. Indeed, was probably the most spectacular interlude of the visit, compared with the blander delights of the programme consisting solely of gymnastic displays and music performed by pupils from six of Perth's schools.

From here the royal couple were driven to the Council House where the official welcomings took place. To the left of the dais on which they stood, children held a hand-painted sign saying, "Please talk to us, Princess Di," and she turned to them as soon as the formalities were over. It

marked the start of the longest, best-received and most boisterous walkabout they had yet undertaken, the crowd almost beside itself with excitement. For once it took the form of a procession in which they walked together in the centre of the roadway, only occasionally darting out toward the crowd to accept toys and posies. Nevertheless the Princess received bouquets which filled the arms of four attendant policewomen, while among Prince Charles'gifts were two jars of Vegemite and a kiss from a 16-year-old student.

That afternoon the Prince and
Princess attended a garden
party in the superbly
landscaped grounds of
Government House. Tropical
palms dominated huge catering
marquees and a military band
serenaded 5,500 guests who
waited in snaking lines for their
glimpse of the royal couple.

The Prince and Princess left Perth, delayed by a cyclonic downpour for over thirty minutes, for Bunbury on 8th April. Thirteen thousand schoolchildren were at the Hands Memorial Oval to provide a well-rehearsed

welcome, highlighted by the presentation of a bouquet by six-year-old Bridget Ryan, and an articulate address from Ian Rummery who affirmed that the diverse ethnic groups in this region of varied backgrounds were "united in the wish to see and welcome you both." In the bright weather, the Princess donned sunglasses, and her one sneeze turned out not to be the herald of a developing chill, despite a breeze which, during Prince Charles' speech, swept his notes away and caused an audible swear. The Mayor of Bunbury reserved a more formal welcome at a small garden party later that morning.

The tiny, unpretentious, brick church of St Paul, Holbrook was the Prince and Princess' venue for Holy Communion on 10th April. Sidesmen on duty outside ticked off the names of local arrivals, after which a lone bellringer rang a lone bell for less than thirty seconds, to call to worship the faithful already in attendance! An electric organ, borrowed from a neighbouring church to replace one that had broken down, was carted hastily and unceremoniously into the building shortly before the royal visitors arrived. During their walkabout afterwards the Princess received a boomerang made, "expressly for Prince William."

The unwritten rule that Brisbane can beat all other Australian royal welcomes persisted when the royal couple entered the Queensland capital on 11th April. The new Queen Street Mall was thick with frenzied well-wishers, and despite a heat of 28° C, the Prince and Princess stuck to their original plan to walk the whole distance to City Hall.

That evening the Prince and Princess arrived at the Crest Hotel, Brisbane for one of the last receptions of their tour. The Princess sparkled in her superb array of Saudi-Arabian sapphires.

Queensland's rural industries provided something different on 12th April. The royal couple met workers at the Yandina Ginger Factory, travelled by nut-mobile at Palmwoods' Macadamia Nut Plant and toured the Sunshine Plantation in a sunshine-yellow train.

It may have been tempting fate to sign off the Australian tour with a visit to Melbourne, with its strong and vocal republican contingent, but even here the Prince and Princess easily won the day. After visiting a typical suburban family in their apartment at Altona, they went on to one of their most hectic walkabouts ever. Almost 200,000 people, over a dozen deep in places, packed the Bourke Street Mall which Prince Charles officially opened. There he announced that most of the thousands of presents given to Prince William would be shared among children in Australian orphanages.

During the walkabout, Prince Charles was kissed on the cheek, and his wife was more gallantly greeted by three members of Melbourne University's Trinity Royal Society. They had been waiting for five hours. "You all deserve a good night's rest," she told them.

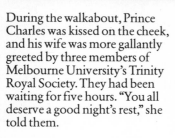

The threat of a protest by IRA sympathisers materialised on the evening of 14th April, when 150 demonstrators gave the royal couple a noisy reception on arrival at Melbourne's Concert Hall for a variety concert. A touching contrast was provided inside by a silent performance of songs "sung" entirely in sign language by a group of deaf children.

After the performance, the Prince and Princess met the artistes, together with members of the Victorian Cabinet and dozens of other distinguished guests, in the three-tiered foyer. It was difficult to deny that the Princess, with her spectacular long, pink dress was, as she had so often been during the past month, the star of the show.

The royal train took the Prince and Princess to the old gold-mining town of Ballarat on 15th April to meet the locals during a half-hour walkabout. The breezy conditions made it difficult for the Princess to keep her dignity, but enlivened a spectacular Chinese dragon dance which she and Prince Charles watched from a hotel balcony in Bendigo later.

At Sovereign Hill they were given a welcome 1850's-style: top hats and crinolines abounded, a police trooper in period costume threatened to arrest them as "a wanted couple newly arrived in the Colony," and they travelled—Prince Charles aloft—in a Cobb & Co. stagecoach.

Only once had the Australians seen Prince William. Now, on 16th April, his penultimate day among them, he was shown off again by his parents at Melbourne Airport, looking healthy, contented and bronzed.

The Princess of Wales saved the best till last. Her cream and silver ball gown, close-fitting and leaving one shoulder completely bare, was a stunner. For once the word "sexy" was as respectable as the occasion—a glittering dinner-dance at the Melbourne Hilton Hotel on the evening of 16th April.

Precisely four weeks after arriving at Alice Springs, the Prince and Princess boarded a RNZAF aircraft and waved farewell to Australia. For Prince Charles his ninth visit presented no problems, but his wife knew from the start that all eyes would be on her and that she must succeed. She not only succeeded, she overwhelmed. Crowds everywhere enveloped her, fixing hopes and pleas on a single

glimpse or word. She was everything to everybody, regardless of age, wealth, position or even loyalty. Prince Charles played no second fiddle, proving an inconspicuous guiding light, prompting his wife by nods, winks and gentle touches through a hundred changes of direction and pace. Together they were an efficient—and popular—team.

First English edition published by Colour Library International Ltd.
© 1983 Illustrations and Text: Colour Library International Ltd.
99 Park Avenue, New York, N.Y. 10016, U.S.A.
Distributed by Crown Publishers, Inc.
h g f e d c b a
Colour separations by Reprocolor Llovet, Barcelona, Spain.
Printed and bound in Barcelona, Spain by Cayfosa and EUROBINDER
ISBN 0-517-421313
CRESCENT 1983